Published by Creative Education
123 South Broad Street
Mankato, Minnesota 56001

Creative Education is an imprint of
The Creative Company.

Art direction by Rita Marshall
Design by The Design Lab
Photographs by Affordable Photo Stock (Francis &
Donna Caldwell), Corbis (Ralph A. Clevenger, D.
Robert & Lorri Franz, Stephen Frink, Gallo Images,
Eric & David Hosking, Steve Kaufman), The Image
Finders (Alan Chapman, Rob Curtis, David Haas,
Carl A. Stimac), JLM Visuals (Peggy Morsch), KAC
Productions (Larry Ditto, John & Gloria Tveten), Tom
Myers, James P. Rowan, Tom Stack & Associates (David
Fleetham, Barbara Gerlach, John Gerlach, Michael
Nolan, Ed Robinson, Inga Spence), Visuals Unlimited
(Jeff J. Daly, G. G. Hartley)

Library of Congress Cataloging-in-Publication Data

Hoff, Mary King.
Communication / by Mary Hoff.
p. cm. – (World of wonder)
Summary: Discusses various forms of communication
in the natural world, with an emphasis on such animals
as the red-winged blackbird, European minnow, and
elephant.
ISBN 1-58341-238-7
1. Animal communication–Juvenile literature. [1. Animal
communication.] I. Title.

QL776 .H64 2002
591.59–dc21   2001047887

First Edition

9 8 7 6 5 4 3 2 1

cover & page 1: courting albatrosses
page 2: a peacock's courtship display
page 3: hippopotamus mates

Creative Education presents

WORLD OF WONDER

COMMUNICATION

BY MARY HOFF

Insects that flash lights to tell others where they are 🕷 Mammals whose posture says, "I'm boss!" 🐀 Snakes whose colors warn other creatures to stay away 🐍 Bees that dance and birds that sing ❋ The world is full of creatures that **communicate** in various ways.

COMMUNICATION MEANS DIFFERENT things to different people. In this book, it is defined as a process in which one living thing provides information that causes another to do something. Communication is an **adaptation**—a characteristic or ability that helps creatures to stay alive and pass life along to another generation.

A zebra snorts and stomps to show who's boss

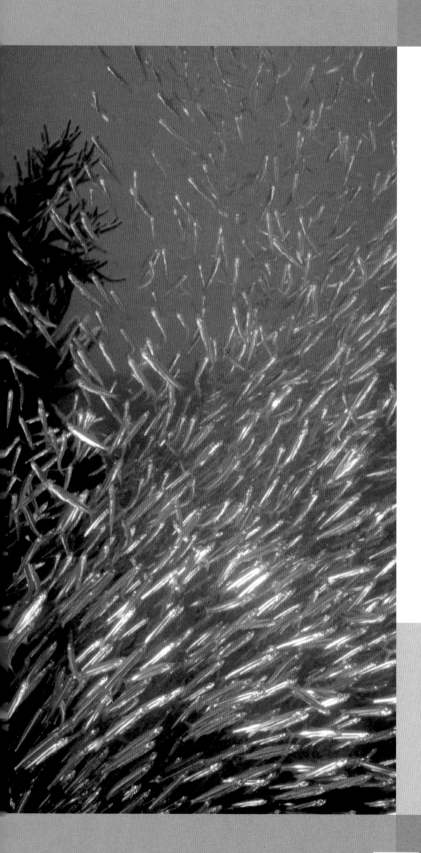

WATCH OUT!

When a fish or other predator takes a bite out of a European minnow, the minnow releases a chemical called an alarm **pheromone** that alerts its neighbors to danger. Other minnows nearby dash about in the water, then cluster together and flee. Many other species of fish are also known to give off alarm pheromones.

NATURE NOTE: *The Austrian scientist who discovered the alarm pheromone of the European minnow called it "Schreckstoff," which translates to "scary stuff" in English.*

All over the world, other animals give warning signals, too. Foraging ostriches in Africa call out if they see an enemy, such as a lion or chee-tah, approaching. The chin-chilla of South America gives a warning whistle when it feels threatened. North American white-tailed deer flash their "flags"—the white undersides of their tails—and snort when they sense danger.

In Africa, vervet monkeys make different warning sounds for different dangers. If a

monkey makes a sound that means "eagle," other monkeys look up. If it makes a sound that means "snake," its companions act to avoid danger in the grass.

NATURE NOTE: *A vervet monkey's vocabulary includes at least three dozen different sounds.*

Ostriches use vocal calls to warn of danger

PLANTS AND INSECTS

Some plants communicate when they are threatened, too. In experiments, scientists have found that sagebrush leaves that are injured release an alarm chemical into the air. Nearby tobacco plants that sense the chemical warning produce a chemical that makes them less **palatable** to plant-eaters.

♣ When tobacco plants are munched on by tobacco bud-worms, they release a batch of airborne chemicals that seems to attract wasps. The wasps fly

Tobacco plants use chemicals to summon help

in and lay their eggs inside the budworms. After they hatch, the young wasps eat the bud-worms, thereby helping the tobacco plants.

🕷 Lima bean plants nibbled by spider mites give off special chemicals, too. When other lima bean plants sense the chemicals, they also produce chemicals. The chemicals help to protect the plants by mak-

NATURE NOTE: *Scientists know of at least 15 plant species that produce chemicals that alert predatory insects to the presence of prey, such as insect larvae or mites.*

11   *Wasps help plants by eating pesky budworms*

ing them less tasty. They also attract other mites that eat the bothersome spider mites.

🌿 Plants communicate with insects to get help in making seeds. Brightly colored flowers and a sweet scent attract **pollinators** by letting them know that the plant contains **nectar**. Some plants attract pollinators using colors humans can't see. When viewed under a special light, primrose and gentian flowers show dark markings not visible in daylight. These markings say "Right this way!" to insects that can see ultraviolet light.

Many flowers use color and smell to attract bees

FOLLOW ME

Food is an important reason to communicate. When an ant finds a speck of jelly on a kitchen counter, it heads for its nest, leaving a pheromone trail behind it. Its nest mates then follow the trail to find the jelly.

❋ Honeybees have a fancy system of communicating about food. When a scout bee finds nectar, she flies to the hive and dances. If the nectar is nearby, she dances in a circle. If the food source is distant, she walks in a pattern that looks like a figure eight. The direction of the figure eight indicates the direction of the food source. The time she spends waggling her body between the two circles indicates the distance to the food. Other bees then fly off to help harvest the treasure.

NATURE NOTE: *Honeybees use nectar to make honey. They store the honey in their hives to use as food during the winter.*

The honeyguide, an African bird, and a badger-like mammal called a ratel use communication to find food together. When the honeyguide spots a bees' nest it can't reach, it makes a chattering sound that attracts a ratel. It then leads the ratel to the hive. The ratel breaks into the nest, and both animals feast on the honey.

NATURE NOTE: *The species name of the honeybee,* mellifera, *means "honey-bearing."*

THIS IS MINE!

Early in the spring, a male red-winged blackbird sits on a cat-tail stalk. Flashing the bright red patch on his wings, he calls, "kok-karee!" He flies to a willow branch and sings again. Then he swoops to another cattail and does the same thing. The bird is telling the world about his **territory**. When he flies around, it is as though he is drawing a dotted line around the space he has claimed for his own.

🕊 Many of the bird songs heard in the spring are the

A red-winged blackbird claims his territory

NATURE NOTE: *The brown thrasher, a member of the bird family known as mimic thrushes, can sing more than 1,000 different songs.*

songs of birds defending territories. These songs help keep too many birds from nesting in one area. They also help ensure that the strongest, healthiest males are the ones that mate and pass their genes along to the next generation.

🐿 Mammals also use communication to set up and defend territories. Many mark their space by urinating, defecating, or leaving scents from **scent glands** around the border of their territory.

GROUP TALK

Members of many species that live or travel with others of their own kind communicate information about themselves to others. A wolf uses various signals to let other members of its pack know how important it is. A dominant wolf will stand with its head and tail up. A subordinate wolf may crouch and whine. These signals help keep the group orderly, so that group members don't have to fight to see who's boss.

☾ Elephants communicate in

NATURE NOTE: *At night, kangaroo rats thump their feet on the ground to let other kangaroo rats know where they are.*

The kangaroo rat communicates with its feet

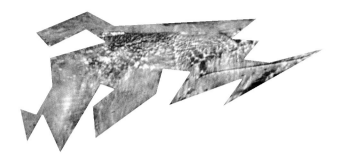

many ways. They may touch each other reassuringly with their trunks. Sometimes they give off rumbles too low for humans to hear. Scientists think these rumbles help elephants coordinate their activities over long distances.

🌢 Whales and dolphins are famous for the many sounds they make to communicate. Some of these sounds let others of the same species know where and who they are. Others are warning calls.

NATURE NOTE: *One whale was recorded singing a single song for 22 hours without stopping!*

Dolphins "talk" using high-pitched sounds

GET-TOGETHERS

In the fall, some birds use communication to gather together. The gold-finches' autumn song, for example, brings the finches together before they start out on their annual flight south to warmer wintering grounds.

Western pine beetles burrow into ponderosa pine trees and eat tunnels into the wood. When they find a nice tree to call home, they give off chemicals that attract other western pine beetles. But when things start getting crowded, the beetles release a different chemical. This chemical discourages

Songs bring birds together for fall migrations

new guests. They have traded their "welcome" sign for a "no vacancy" sign.

🜲 Baby quail use communication to coordinate their activities even while they are still in eggs. The unhatched quail make clicking sounds when they are about ready to hatch that encourage the other young to develop faster. This helps them to all hatch at about the same time, making it easier for the mother to care for the young quail.

Baby quail communicate even before they hatch

MAKING BABIES

A very important function of communication is to help living things reproduce.

This kind of communication is sometimes very simple. In brown algae, the

female **gametes** give off a chemical that attracts male gametes. This helps the

cells to find each other in the ocean.

🐾 Many animals call, display fancy body parts, dance, or do other things to let

others know they are ready to breed. Insects such as moths and fruit flies sing

songs or release chemicals to attract mates. Crickets and frogs chirp to each other. Male peregrine falcons perform aerial acrobatics to impress prospective mates.

🕷 On hot summer nights, fireflies flash signals that say, "I'm here! I'm the same species as you and ready to mate!" Different species of fireflies have different flashes.

NATURE NOTE: *Male prairie chickens gather in the spring to dance, make loud sounds, and inflate bright-colored neck sacs. Females watch and then choose a mate from among the dancers.*

Fireflies flash signals at night to find mates

LEAVE ME ALONE

Yellow and black is a common color combination in nature. It often means that a creature (for example, a bee, frog, or salamander) is dangerous or bothersome. Red is a common warning color, too. Coral snakes have bright yellow, black, and red stripes. They also have a poisonous bite. The colors warn predators to stay away.

NATURE NOTE: *Kingsnakes have markings similar to those of coral snakes. So, even though kingsnakes aren't poisonous, predators avoid them.*

A coral snake's bright coloration is a warning

A honeybee's stripes tell enemies it can sting

Animals also communicate "don't mess with me" messages to other species through behavior. The snarling of wolves and the rattling of rattlesnakes are warnings to people or other animals to go away.

Sometimes animals scare potential enemies away by bluffing. Some moths, such as the io moth and the polyphemus moth, have round spots on their wings. Scientists believe that these spots may startle or frighten enemies because they look like eyes.

NATURE NOTE: *Some male moths can smell females that are ready to mate more than a mile (1.6 km) away!*

Killdeer are birds that nest on the ground. When a predator approaches a killdeer nest, the mother killdeer moves away, dragging her wing on the ground as though she is injured. Seeing an easy meal, the enemy follows her. When she has led the predator far enough from the nest, the killdeer flies away. Her bluff often saves her eggs or offspring.

NATURE NOTE: *The white-tailed deer's flag may tell an enemy it's been spotted. Because it knows it can no longer surprise the deer, the hungry predator may not bother to attack.*

MANY CONNECTIONS

From cells that ooze chemicals to whales that sing in the sea, communication is all around us. It helps living things find food, find mates, avoid predators, and carry out other functions essential to life.

✳ Communication is just one way in which living things interact with each other. The more we learn about nature, the more we see that living things are connected to each other in countless ways. By considering the impact our actions have on the environment and its wild creatures, we can help ensure the future health and beauty of this amazing world, this world of wonder.

NATURE NOTE: *Some of the low-pitched sounds that whales make can carry more than 100 miles (161 km) through the water.*

WORDS TO KNOW

An **adaptation** is a characteristic that contributes to a living thing's ability to survive or reproduce.

To **communicate** is to provide understandable information to another living thing.

Gametes are special cells that combine to make new living things. Eggs and sperm are both gametes.

Genes are the parts of chromosomes within an animal's cells that carry the information needed to make it what it is. They are passed from one generation to the next.

Plants attract pollinators with a sweet liquid called **nectar**.

Something that is **palatable** is good to eat.

A **pheromone** is a chemical that carries messages from one animal to another.

Pollinators are animals that carry the male plant gametes (in pollen) to female plant gametes so they can combine to make a new plant.

Scent glands are special body parts that release odors animals use to communicate.

An animal's **territory** is the space it defends for its own use.

INDEX